Grill Cookbo Beginners

MW00934687

Learn To Make 50+Delicious Recipes Under Your Grill And Make your Family Gatherings Joyful

FRANKLIN BURROWS

Contents

Introduction..5

CHAPTER 1: Grilling Benefits and Tips 7

1. *Advantages of Grilling* 7

2. *Grilling Tips* 12

CHAPTER 2: Grilled Cooking Pork Recipes 14

1. *Chili-Rubbed Ribs* 14

2. *Grilled Pork Chops* 15

3. *Grilled Rib Eye with Sweet-Hot Pepper Sauce* 16

4. *Pork Tenderloin with Cherry Salsa Mole* 17

5. *Baby Back Ribs* 18

6. *Spicy Pork Skewers* 19

7. *Smoky Grilled Pork Chops* 20

8. *Smoky Grilled Pork Loin Chops* 21

9. *BBQ Pork Chops* 22

10. *Smoked n Grilled Pork Loin with Summer Spice Dry Rub* 22

11. *Texas Two-Step Pork Chops* 23

12. *Pork Chop Marinade Recipe* 24

CHAPTER 3: Grilled Burgers and Sandwiches Recipes 26

1. *Italian Sausage Sandwiches* 26

2. *Teriyaki Portabella Mushroom Burger with Garlic Mayonnaise* 27

3. *Cajun Sirloin Burgers* 28

4. *Grilled Eggplant and Pepper Goat Cheese Sandwiches* 29

5. *Grilled Branzino with Preserved Lemon Gremolata* 30

6. *Grilled Chicken Shawarma Recipe* 31

7. *Thai Turkey Burgers with Crunchy Asian Slaw* 32

8. *Grilled Lamb Burger with Harissa Aioli* 34

9. *Grilled Naan with Garlic Scape Chutney* 35

10. *Sprouted Lentil Burgers (grill able and vegan)* 36

11. *Grilled Pizza with Gorgonzola, Figs, Balsamic onions* 38

12. *Healthy Burger Bowls* 39

13. *Lamb Kofta Lettuce Wraps* 40

CHAPTER 4: Grilled Chicken Recipes **42**

   1.   Grilled Sambal Chicken 42

   2.   Best Grilled Chicken Breast 43

   3.   Grilled chicken 44

   4.   Easy Grilled Chicken Breast 45

   5.   Peruvian Chicken with Spicy Peruvian Green Sauce 46

   6.   Sticky Barbecue Chicken 48

   7.   Chicken Breasts with Romesco Sauce 49

   8.   Cuban Mojo Chicken Legs 51

   9.   Buttermilk Brined Rotisserie Chicken 52

   10.   Chicken Drumsticks with Barbecue Sauce 53

CHAPTER 5: Grilled Salads Recipes **55**

   1.   Grilled Corn 55

   2.   Grilled Romaine Salad with Corn, Fava Beans and Avocado 56

   3.   Grilled Romaine Salad with Maitake Mushrooms 57

   4.   Chipotle Grilled Chicken Salad with Grilled Corn, Peppers and Quinoa 59

   5.   Summer Nicoise Salad with Grilled Fish 60

   6.   Mango & Grilled Chicken Salad 62

CHAPTER 6: Grilled Seafood Recipes **63**

   1.   Grilled Salmon Tzatziki Bowl 63

   2.   Pineapple chipotle shrimp skewers 64

   3.   Grilled Salmon with Pickled Huckleberry Relish 65

   4.   Cedar Planked Salmon with Lemon Butter 66

   5.   Grilled Oysters with Pecorino and Shaved Bottarga 68

   6.   Grilled Caesar Salmon Foil Packets 69

   7.   Lemony Shrimp & Tomatoes 70

   8.   Garlic Butter Salmon 71

   9.   Easy Grilled Sesame Salmon 72

   10.   Easy Grilled Sesame Shrimp with Shishito Peppers 73

   11.   Grilled Shrimp with Oregano and Lemon 74

   12.   Citrus-Soy Squid 75

Conclusion **76**

Introduction

Grilling is something we all have grown up seeing our parents do since we can recall. We used to be mesmerized by looking at those fat hotdogs plump up & split when we were kids. Remember the aroma of the beef from those juicy, thick burgers, all the fat dripping onto the glowing red coal with a hiss, fire shot, & blue smoke curled around sizzling edges? It's now entertaining to watch your children or grandchildren's faces light up as they see you flip the burgers with showmanship and style. Grilling could be considered a natural instinct. It's in our bloodstream almost from the moment we're born. Grilling is described as a dry, fast cooking method that employs a substantial amount of radiant, direct heat in the scientific version. Direct conduction heating is used when frying in a griddle or pan, whereas thermal radiation is used when grilling. Grilling temperatures frequently exceed 260°C or 500°F, creating a quick-cooking method that must be closely monitored. Otherwise, the perfectly cooked hotdogs will quickly turn into road flares. The browning of proteins and sugars on meat and vegetables, which creates that beautiful coloration and additional flavor profile, is what surely makes grilled food taste better. Maillard reaction occurs when the foods reach temps above 155°C or 310°F, & it causes browning. True grilling consists of cooking foods on an open-wire grid with fire either below or above the food. Broiling is the term we use when the source of heat is above, yet it still falls under our definition of grilling. The temperature and cooking time are the main differences between grilling & barbecuing.

Grilling involves quick cooking on high heat, whereas barbecuing involves slow cooking for a long period of time using indirect, low heat. Every cooking method usually necessitates the use of different equipment. The quality of the meat is another substantial difference between the two cooking methods. Tough & fatty meats require a slow, long cooking process in order to break the collagen & other tissues down, resulting in juicy, tender meat. That's why we grill with larger, less expensive cuts. Tender or Lean meat, chicken, & seafood, on the other hand, require rapid cooking at high temperatures to reach a safe internal temperature without drying out. The Mycenaean civilization in ancient Greece, around 1600 B.C., was the first to demonstrate that man already knew about throwing a tailgate party. Rectangular ceramic trays were discovered during the archaeological excavations. Julie Hruby, a Dartmouth College assistant professor for classics, experimented by reconstructing the ancient trays of clay in order to better understand their function. They turned out to be heavy but ceramic portable grills with a tray that held coals for cooking skewered meat. In Greece, it's known as souvlaki, and in other parts of the world, it's known as ShishKa Bob. Weight wasn't an issue back then because they had oxen and slaves. Thankfully, we now have pickup trucks, SUVs, & lightweight metal grills, which we may take with us wherever we go. Although your oven has a good set of many racks, may you grill inside it? You can't do it. Grilling, on the other hand, involves radiant heat rather than flavor-inducing coals or flame. Your oven either bakes or roasts food. Consider the hot stone method, which is used by survivalists, hardcore woodsmen, and cavemen. You heat a flat rock until it's smoking hot, then move it to one side of the fire to cook the meat. Is it time to fire up the grill? It isn't the case. The

heat is generated by the stone rather than the coals or fire. Cooking in a skillet or with the famous George Foreman Grill is the same. It's an electric skillet with two sides. There was no smoke, no fire, and no enjoyment. Grilling is simple and requires no special equipment. There are only three things you need to grill: meat, grill, and fire. Of course, there's a lot more to learn, including many grilling tips and tricks that will help us improve our game, but those three things are the most important. Nothing enhances the flavor of meat, quite like fire and smoke. That's all there is to it. Rekindle your childhood memories by firing up the grill.

CHAPTER 1: Grilling Benefits and Tips

The grill's a piece of the cooking equipment with an open grate or rack as the cooking surface and underneath, a heat source. The heat source could be open flame (charcoal or gas) or electric, depending on the type of grill. Because food is directly cooked on the grill's grate or rack, the best foods for grilling are meats & poultry, though seafood, firm fish, and vegetables can also be cooked on a grill. Because the grills cook with dry heat and great temperature, meats cooked on one must be tender cut of the meat, & marinating can help to keep moisture in the meat. Grill marks from the grate or rack are one of the characteristics of the food that is cooked on the grill. This effect may be achieved by using the grill pan, which is a specially designed pan. Although The raised ridges on the grill pan may form grill markings, it isn't actually grilling.

1. Advantages of Grilling

Listed below are the various advantages of grilled food.

No need for butter

Margarine is a high-fat, high-calorie food. It has a strong flavor and is frequently used as a spread as well as in food preparation and cooking. It's been linked to coronary artery disease for a long time. Whatever the case may be, it is currently regarded as reliable as long as it is used with caution. However, if you're concerned about your health and your eating habits, it's best to avoid it at all costs. Also, if you want delectable food without the use of spread, barbecue the food because all

of the juices extracted from the organic products, vegetables and meats just leak out & make them much more delectable. Eggplant, pineapples, romaine lettuce, and zucchini are all options. Grilling no longer necessitates the use of butter. All of the juices from the meats and vegetables ooze out, making everything taste better. This also entails consuming fewer calories. Furthermore, it reduces the intake of harmful substances in your body.

Lifts social relationships

Grilling is a great way to spend time with family and friends. You can do it at home or outside, such as on the beach or at a bus stop. It will also motivate you to take action that is beneficial to your overall health and well-being. You can do a variety of things while grilling food, such as play sports with your children.

Grilling removes fat

Grilling gets rid of a lot of fat, including saturated fats, that raise cholesterol levels. The fat is rendered and then consumed by the heat source. In some foods, such as a good steak, grilling rare will not remove as much fat as grilling medium will, but fat around the edges will be reduced. The other half of the equation dates back to the dawn of time when the first primitive humans discovered fire and soon discovered that cooked meat tasted better than raw meat. Cooking food is almost as old as the art of taming fire. Something inherent in a human's DNA must transport the taste buds back to a time when cooking over an open fire was the norm. Grilling also beats out deep frying in terms of calories and saturated fat, lowering overall calories and cholesterol while increasing flavor and satisfaction. Grilling is healthier because the meat does not sit in the fat and grease as compared to different ways of cooking, such as roasting or frying. Grilled food contains less oil and fat. Furthermore, the majority of grilled foods are cooked in their own juices, making them healthier.

More nutritious veggies

It is Because grilling vegetables takes less time than cooking them in a traditional oven, they tend to retain much more of the natural nutrition. In the cooking water, stewed or boiled vegetables leave most of their flavor, also their mineral and vitamin content. Roasted vegetables, on the other hand, keep their texture and color while gaining flavor and nutrients.

You can have multiple flavors

Grilling over various types of wood imparts distinct flavors to the food. Grilling does not require frying oil, whereas frying does. When compared to grilling, steaming does not produce the same natural flavors.

You can grill literally any food

On the grill, you can cook any type of meat, fruit, or vegetable. Other specialties include pineapple smothered in brown sugar and cooked over an open fire, which is a desert.

It is a lot of fun

You can get a great wood-smoke flavor out of your food. Using a good marinade and basting your meat or veggies as you slowly grill can transform ordinary chicken or squash into something truly special and delectable. It's also a great reason to spend some time outside in the sun around the grill.

Nutrient-rich meats

Grilled vegetables aren't the only thing that becomes more nutritious when cooked on the grill. The riboflavin and thiamine content of meat cooked on the grill is higher. B vitamins such as thiamine and riboflavin help the body convert food into energy. Grilled meat or seafood that is completely cooked and not charred over a gas flame is an excellent addition to a healthy diet.

No need for condiments for realizing grilling health benefits

When you grill food, none of the minerals and vitamins in it are lost. Grilling keeps more of these in the food, making it taste better. The grill will seal in moisture, so you won't need to add extra seasonings to get the flavor you want. As a result, you consume fewer calories and eat less unhealthy foods, which otherwise potentially lead to obesity.

Grilling helps preserve nutrients and thus adds to health benefits

Grilling meat is a healthier method of cooking because the nutrients thiamine (Vitamin B1) and riboflavin are preserved (Vitamin B2). Thiamine aids in the breakdown of carbohydrates into energy and the prevention of certain diseases, whereas Riboflavin aids in energy production. Cooking on the grills tends to keep the vegetables and meat soft. Moreover, it helps to preserve the natural flavor.

It kills bacteria

For those who eat meat, grilling over an open fire has the advantage of killing bacteria in the meat. Another is that the fat disappears. This way, you consume fewer calories and are less likely to gain weight. The fine smoke aroma from the charcoal would appeal to vegans, as would the fact that it contains fewer calories in some cases. Instead of roasting the eggplant in vegetable oil in a pan, you can, instead, prepare the eggplant in pieces on thin rods.

Increased physical activity

Grilling can be a social event in your backyard with friends or family. It's a far more relaxed and healthy way to enjoy your food, with kids playing games and adults socializing and drinking wine and beer. Everyone is welcome to participate and have a good time. You can have a few people grill at the same time or even have a healthy grilling competition if you have several grills. You could even request that your friends bring their grills. This gives everyone an opportunity to the creation of happy memories or participation in outdoor activities.

Reduces health risks

When you eat grilled foods, you may get all of the beneficial vitamins and nutrients they contain. It entails the consumption of vegetables, fruits, and meat. You & your family will be healthier & fitter as a result of this. It also aids in the prevention of health problems like heart disease, obesity, stroke, high b.p., & even certain types of cancers. Grilled food contains less fat & calories than pan-fried food. Whether you cook low-fat food, when you're frying it, the food becomes saturated with fat. The meat mostly cooks in the own fat when grilled. This eliminates the need for additional oil, sauce, or condiments, resulting in a reduction in calories and fat.

Low sodium intake

Now, are you aware that you may be consuming extra sodium than the body requires? This is due to the fact that we consume at least seventy % of our sodium from packaged foods and restaurants. Because sodium is added just before you purchase the food, it's difficult to keep track of your sodium intake. You may control the amount of sodium in your food by cooking your food from scratch and grilling it. Grilling produces natural flavors. This, in turn, reduces the use of salt.

No smells inside the house

Grilling keeps the cooking smell outside if you don't want it inside your kitchen or house. Consider how strong the smell of smoked bacon is in your house when you cook it in summers with air conditioning AC on or also in winter with the heat on; grilling it outside would eliminate that.

No heat indoors

You would not want the heat from grilling to be confined inside your home. During the

summer months, and grilling keeps the heat outside. The heat from an oven is trapped in the house for several hours. This may not be much of a bad thing in the winter, but in summers, you want to keep the heat outside of the kitchen. Enjoy the art of grilling by grilling your next meal outside.

2. Grilling Tips

Meat that has been grilled may produce carcinogens, which can cause cancer. Here are some suggestions for grilling that are healthier. When grilling fruits and vegetables, you don't have to worry about these tips because they don't produce carcinogens.

- Remove any excess fat from the meat. When fat drips onto hot charcoal, it ignites, producing cancer-causing smoke. It's critical to get rid of as much fat as possible. Before cooking the chicken, we strongly advise you to remove the skin.

- Marinate meat in antioxidant-rich ingredients such as garlic, onion, lemon juice, cinnamon, turmeric, olive oil (virgin), and beer for a few hours before grilling (Pilsner, non-alcoholic).

- Avoid using lighter fluid and only use natural charcoal. As an alternative to lighter fluids, you can use a paper towel and cooking oil.

- Use an onion to clean the grill grates, then oil them with a paper towel & tongs.

- Instead of well-done, cook the steak medium-rare. When compared to medium-rare steak, well-done steak has three times the amount of carcinogens.

- When grilling, avoid charring your meat too much. When cooking kebabs, you may want to turn them more frequently to ensure even cooking and prevent the meat from burning on one side.

- Charcoal can expose your food to potentially cancer-causing chemicals. The meat must not be overcooked when grilling with charcoal. Also, keep your food away from cigarette smoke. We strongly recommend that you must do your grilling on a gas grill. It is a healthier method of cooking that avoids the use of hazardous chemicals.

- Anything that can be roasted can be grilled. To avoid your dinner drying out, you simply need to be aware of the size of the ingredient and the cooking time required. Grill larger pieces than smaller pieces when it comes to size. For example, instead of cubed steak, grill a whole steak. Meat shrinks as it cooks, and cubes may fall through the grill to the coals or fire. The same can be said for any veggies you grill.

- When grilling, you must use the food thermometer always. It ensures that food is cooked to correct internal temperature & provides you with peace of mind.

- The grill must be heated to 145 degrees Fahrenheit for lamb, veal, beef, and pork.

- You should grill eggs as well as ground beef just at 160 deg F.

- Poultry should be grilled at 165 deg F.

- When extra fat drips onto the heat source, it causes it to flare up. It may result in the formation of cancer-causing P.A.Hs on the food. In addition, the meat might taste "off," & the flames might burn the outside of food before the inside is cooked. Buy the lean meats & remove the skin & excess fat from poultry to avoid flare-ups. Also, keep a water bottle nearby to put out any stray flames.

- Cross-contamination must be avoided. This is accomplished by using utensils, cutting platters, and boards to separate raw and cooked foods. This holds true for meat, fish, and fruits and vegetables. Marinated foods should be kept refrigerated. Cooking a type of food at one time is recommended, with utensils & cutting boards being washed after each use. Frequently turning food tends to protect from burning.

CHAPTER 2: Grilled Cooking Pork Recipes

Enjoy cooking delicious pork on your grill for your friends and families.

1. Chili-Rubbed Ribs

Preparation time

1 hour 30 minutes

Servings

8 persons

Ingredients

We have listed below the ingredients that would be required by you for cooking the healthy and tasty meal:

- 3 teaspoons ground cumin
- 2/3 cup ketchup
- 1/3 cup lemon juice
- 1-1/2 teaspoons minced fresh gingerroot
- 2 teaspoons garlic powder
- 1 teaspoon salt

- 3 tablespoons packed brown sugar

- 2 tablespoons paprika

- 2 tablespoons chili powder

- 6 pounds pork baby back ribs

- 1 cup reduced-sodium soy sauce

- 1 cup packed brown sugar

Instructions

Given below are the detailed instructions for cooking this tasty meal. You need to follow these instructions in the given order.

- Combine the main ingredients and rub them all over the ribs. Refrigerate for 30 minutes, covered.

- Wrap big pieces of thick foil around the rib racks and seal tightly. It is to be grilled for one to one and a half hours, covered, over indirect medium heat until tender.

- Combine glaze ingredients in a large saucepan; cook, uncovered, over medium heat for 6-8 minutes, or till heated through and sugar is dissolved, stirring occasionally.

- Remove the ribs from the foil with care. Brush some of the glazes on the ribs and place them over direct heat. You have to cook it, properly covered, at medium heat for twenty-five to thirty minutes, turning as well as brushing ribs with remaining glaze as needed.

2. Grilled Pork Chops

Preparation time

30 minutes

Servings

4 persons

Ingredients

We have listed below the ingredients that would be required by you for cooking the healthy and tasty meal:

- Four bone-in pork chops one and a half-inch thick, center-cut, 8 ounces each

- Freshly ground black pepper

- Kosher salt

- Dry Rub Seasoning for Pork

Instructions

Given below are the detailed instructions for cooking this tasty meal. You need to follow these instructions in the given order.

- Aluminum foil should be used for lining the rimmed sheet pan.

- Refrigerate pork chops for 1 to 24 hours after liberally seasoning them with kosher salt.

- Remove the chops from the fridge thirty minutes before grilling when ready to cook.

- Season the pork chops with kosher salt and freshly ground black pepper.

- Heat the coals until they are completely covered in ash, then push them to cover half of the grill. Place the grate on the grill and cover it for 5 minutes. The grill will be able to preheat as a result of this.

- The grilling grate should be cleaned and oiled.

- Cook the pork chops for 3-5 minutes on the hot side of the grill, or till golden brown on the bottom side. Turn the chops over again and cook for another 3-5 minutes, or until the other side is browned.

- Place the chops on the cool side of the grill, bone side up, facing the flames. Cover, cook, as well as flip the chops in 1-minute intervals unless an instant-read meat thermometer is inserted into the thickest part of the pork chop registers 135°F. Then take out the chops from the grill and set them aside. The internal temperature of the meat should rise to 145°F after 10 minutes of resting after cooking.

3. Grilled Rib Eye with Sweet-Hot Pepper Sauce

Preparation time

50 minutes

Servings

2 persons

Ingredients

We have listed below the ingredients that would be required by you for cooking the healthy and tasty meal:

- 1 1/2 tbsp. Finely chopped parsley

- 1/2 lb. Of beef fat, dry-aged, trimmed

- One (24-oz.) Prime steak rib-eye, dry-aged & bone-in

- One tbsp. Oregano, finely chopped

- One teaspoon fish sauce

- Four cherry peppers or pickled calabrian, seeded

- 1⁄4 cup canola oil

- Black pepper freshly ground to taste

- 6 cloves garlic, peeled

- 2 tbsp. Olive oil

- Four sweet pickled cherry peppers, seeded

- Kosher salt or smoked sea and sea weed salt, to taste

Instructions

Given below are the detailed instructions for cooking this tasty meal. You need to follow these instructions in the given order.

- In a 1-quart saucepan, heat the canola oil & garlic over medium heat till the garlic's tender, about 4 to 6 minutes. You need to use the food processor, purée the garlic until smooth, discarding the oil. Pulse together the fish sauce, oregano, olive oil, peppers, parsley, salts and pepper to make a thick sauce.

- Set the gas grill to high heat or charcoal grill to high heat; bank coal, or you can turn off one burner. Grill the beef fat for 2 to 3 minutes, flipping once, till slightly charred; transfer to 10″ ovenproof skillet & grill. Then cook for 20 to 30 minutes, or until the fat has melted.

- Season the steak with salt and pepper and grill for 6-8 minutes, flipping one time, until browned. Continue grilling, flipping & basting as required, till slightly charred as well as cooked to the desired consistency, six to eight mins for the medium rare and/or till thermometer (instant-read) reads 125 degrees F. Allow steak to rest for 5 minutes before serving with sauce.

4. Pork Tenderloin with Cherry Salsa Mole

Preparation time

3 hour 30 minutes

Servings

4 persons

Ingredients

We have listed below the ingredients that would be required by you for cooking the healthy and tasty meal:

- 1/4 tsp ground cumin

- 1 green onion, thinly sliced

- 1 tablespoon lime juice

- 1 teaspoon honey

- Salted pumpkin seeds or pepitas

- 1/4 tsp chili powder

- One cup pitted frozen or fresh sweet dark cherries, thawed, finely chopped

- One jalapeno pepper, minced and seeded

- Half-cup peeled jicama, finely chopped

- 2 pork tenderloins (3/4 pound each)

- 1 tablespoon canola oil

- A half teaspoon salt

- One ounce grated semisweet chocolate,

- 2 tbsp fresh cilantro, minced

Instructions

Given below are the detailed instructions for cooking this tasty meal. You need to follow these instructions in the given order.

- Tenderloins should be brushed with oil and seasoned with cumin, chili powder and salt. Then cook, covered, over the medium heat for 15 to 20 minutes, till a thermometer shows 145° F, turning once or twice. Allow for 10 to 15 minutes of resting time.

- Combine the green onion, cherries, jicama, cilantro, jalapeno, lime juice, chocolate, and honey in a mixing bowl. Pork should be sliced and served with cherry salsa as well as pumpkin seeds.

5. Baby Back Ribs

Preparation time

3 hours 30 minutes

Servings

4-6 persons

Ingredients

We have listed below the ingredients that would be required by you for cooking the healthy and tasty meal:

- Four slabs skinned baby back ribs, one and a half to two pounds each

Instructions

Given below are the detailed instructions for cooking this tasty meal. You need to follow these instructions in the given order.

- Preheat the grill. Coals should be lit, and the grill should be covered. When the temperature reaches 230°–250° F, the grill is ready.

- Dry the ribs with paper towels before applying the dry rub to both sides. Place the slabs on the grill rack, over the drip pan, and away from the flames. Cook for 4–6 hours on a covered grill, adding more coals as well as wood as needed. Turn the ribs halfway through cooking.

- Once you can softly pull the ribs apart with gloved hands, they're done. Cut between individual ribs after transferring slabs to a cutting board as well as allowing it to cool slightly. If desired, it can be served with Kansas City Barbecue Sauce.

6. Spicy Pork Skewers

Preparation time

3 hours 30 minutes

Servings

8 persons

Ingredients

We have listed below the ingredients that would be required by you for cooking the healthy and tasty meal:

- 8 garlic cloves, coarsely chopped

- 1Tbsp. black peppercorns

- 1Tbsp. kosher salt, plus more

- 6 dried shiitake mushrooms

- 1 cup Sprite or 7UP

- A half-cup soy sauce

- ⅓ cup cane vinegar

- 2 lb. skinless, boneless pork shoulder

- A half small red onion, thinly sliced

- 12 red Thai chilies, coarsely chopped

- A quarter cup of sugar

Instructions

Given below are the detailed instructions for cooking this tasty meal. You need to follow these instructions in the given order.

- Pork should be frozen on a rimmed baking sheet for 45–60 minutes or till very firm around the edges. Remove the pork from the freezer and thinly slice it. Then use a sharp knife, cut the pieces lengthwise into one-inch to two-inch-wide strips.

- In a large re-sealable plastic bag, soy sauce, combine onion, chilies, garlic, Sprite, vinegar, sugar, peppercorns and one tbsp. Salt. Mushrooms, ground to a powder in a spice mill or mortar and pestle, is whisked into the marinade. Add a few pieces of pork at a time, coating thoroughly so they don't stick together and can absorb the marinade evenly. Chill for 6–8 hours, covered.

- Preheat the grill to medium-high. Remove the pork from the marinade and skewer it. Bring the marinade to a boil in a small saucepan over high heat on the grill. Cook for one minute, skimming any foam that rises to the top. Transfer to a cooler section of the grill.

- You have to season pork gently with salt and cook, uncovered, for 2 minutes or until well-browned. Turn the meat over and baste with the marinade. Continue to grill, turning as well as basting every minute, for another 4 minutes or until the chicken is cooked through as well as browned all over.

7. Smoky Grilled Pork Chops

Preparation time

55 minutes

Servings

4 persons

Ingredients

We have listed below the ingredients that would be required by you for cooking the healthy and tasty meal:

- One tablespoon garlic powder
- 1 teaspoon liquid smoke flavoring
- 4 bone-in pork chops (1/2 to 3/4 inch thick)
- 1 tablespoon onion powder
- 1 tablespoon ground paprika
- 2 teaspoons Worcestershire sauce
- 1 tablespoon seasoned salt
- One teaspoon ground black pepper

Instructions

Given below are the detailed instructions for cooking this tasty meal. You need to follow these instructions in the given order.

- Heat an outdoor grill to medium heat and brush the grate lightly with oil.

- Combine the Worcestershire sauce, seasoned salt, onion powder, black pepper, garlic powder, paprika and smoke flavoring in a mixing bowl and stir well. Rinse the pork chops and season both sides with the spice mixture while they are still wet. Massage the spice, rub it into the meat with your hands and set aside for 10 minutes.

- Grill the chops until they are no longer pink on the inside, approximately 12 minutes per side, over indirect heat. At least 145 degrees Fahrenheit should be read on an instant-read thermometer (63 degrees C). Allow 10 minutes more for the chops to rest before serving.

8. Smoky Grilled Pork Loin Chops

Preparation time

4 hours 45 minutes

Servings

4 persons

Ingredients

We have listed below the ingredients that would be required by you for cooking the healthy and tasty meal:

- Pork loin chops
- Kosher salt
- Brine
- Sixty-four ounces apple juice
- Brown sugar
- Grill Mates Pork Rub

Instructions

Given below are the detailed instructions for cooking this tasty meal. You need to follow these instructions in the given order.

- Trim the fat around the edges that won't penetrate the meat, as well as the thin layer of silver skin beneath the fat.

- Then brine it.

- After heating 32 ounces of apple juice, combine the remaining ingredients, including the remaining apple juice. Pour the brine into a ZipLock bag, insert the chops, and refrigerate for 3 hours after it has cooled.

- Cook at a temperature of 265 degrees Fahrenheit on average

9. BBQ Pork Chops

Preparation time

3 hours 30 minutes

Servings

4-6 persons

Ingredients

We have listed below the ingredients that would be required by you for cooking the healthy and tasty meal:

- Barbecue Sauce
- Smoked Pork Chops

Instructions

Given below are the detailed instructions for cooking this tasty meal. You need to follow these instructions in the given order.

- Low and Slow - the best approach to a juicy chop is to keep it off direct heat and cook it slowly enough to warm it through.
- Brush barbecue sauce on both sides of the smoked chops with a pastry brush.
- After a few minutes, flip the pork chops on the nearest rack to the heat source; the goal is to get a nice set of grill marks on each side without overcooking.
- To fully cook the meat to the proper temperature, move it to the upper rack.
- Then use a meat thermometer to ensure accuracy, based on the thickness of the chops.

10. Smoked n Grilled Pork Loin with Summer Spice Dry Rub

Preparation time

1 day 3 hours

Servings

12 persons

Ingredients

We have listed below the ingredients that would be required by you for cooking the healthy and tasty meal:

- 6 cups water
- 2 tbsp black peppercorns
- 2 fresh thyme sprigs

- ½ cup brown sugar

- 2 tsp salt

- 4 pounds loin pork (center) roast

- 4 to 6 tablespoon Smoking Summers Spice BBQ Dry Rub

- Three cloves garlic, chopped

Instructions

Given below are the detailed instructions for cooking this tasty meal. You need to follow these instructions in the given order.

- Combine brine ingredients in a mixing bowl and stir till the salt and brown sugar are completely dissolved.

- Fill a glass or plastic container halfway with water and pour the brine over the loin roast. The brine must completely cover the meat.

- Then Place inside the refrigerator for 24 to 48 hours to allow flavors to meld.

- Using paper towels, pat meat dry. Apply a generous amount of Summer Spices Dry Rub to the loin roast. If you want to let all the flavor of spices penetrate the meat, leave it for two to eight hours prior to actually grilling it.

- Barbecue for up to three hours or much longer at indirect heat at 250 degrees F, depending on thickness and size of roast. Then take a meat thermometer so that you can make sure the center of the pork loin reaches 160 F. It is the best way to ensure it is fully cooked.

11. Texas Two-Step Pork Chops

Preparation time

4 hours 10 minutes

Servings

4 persons

Ingredients

We have listed below the ingredients that would be required by you for cooking the healthy and tasty meal:

- A quarter cup red wine vinegar

- 1 teaspoon kosher salt

- 4 pork chops (one inch thick)

- 2 tablespoons Worcestershire sauce

- 1 tablespoon minced garlic

- Cup catsup
- ¼ cup apple juice
- A quarter cup extra virgin olive oil
- 1 tablespoon hot sauce
- One tablespoon chili powder

Instructions

Given below are the detailed instructions for cooking this tasty meal. You need to follow these instructions in the given order.

- Except for the pork, combine all of the ingredients in a large mixing bowl.
- Then half-cup marinade is to be set aside for basting.
- Place the chops in a re-sealable bag with the rest of the marinade.
- Close the bag and turn the meat to coat it.
- Refrigerate for four hours before serving.
- Allow 30 minutes for the chops to come back to room temperature.
- Drain, discard marinade, as well as grill over medium heat charcoal, basting and occasionally turning, till just barely pink (10 minutes).

12. Pork Chop Marinade Recipe

Preparation time

50 minutes

Servings

4 persons

Ingredients

We have listed below the ingredients that would be required by you for cooking the healthy and tasty meal:

- ¼ c. reduced-sodium soy sauce
- 3 cloves garlic minced
- 4 bone-in pork chops
- 2 Tbsp Worcestershire sauce
- 2 Tbsp brown sugar
- ¼ c. extra virgin olive oil

- 1 tsp salt
- A half tsp ground black pepper

Instructions

Given below are the detailed instructions for cooking this tasty meal. You need to follow these instructions in the given order.

- Except for the pork chops, whisk together all of the ingredients in a small bowl.
- Place the pork chops in a re-sealable zip-lock bag or a large mixing bowl, as well as pour the marinade over them. Squeeze out as much air as possible and seal the bag.
- Then it is to be marinated for a minimum of two hours or overnight in the refrigerator.
- Preheat a grill pan or a grill to medium heat. Place the pork chops on the grill or in a skillet. Remove and discard any remaining marinade.
- Grill for 4-5 minutes on each side over medium heat, till a thermometer inserted in the center of the meat, registers 145 degrees F. Remove the grill from the heat.
- Allow 3-5 minutes for the pork chops to rest before serving.

CHAPTER 3: Grilled Burgers and Sandwiches Recipes

Enjoy cooking delicious burgers and sandwiches for special occasions.

3. Italian Sausage Sandwiches

Preparation time

1 hour 7 minutes

Servings

4 persons

Ingredients

We have listed below the ingredients that would be required by you for cooking the healthy and tasty meal:

- 4 garlic cloves, minced

- 20 uncooked Italian sausage links

- 20 sandwich buns

- Shredded part-skim mozzarella cheese
- One can (15 ounces) tomato sauce
- 1 can (12 ounces) tomato paste
- One cup water
- 1 tablespoon sugar
- 4 large green peppers, thinly sliced
- A half-cup chopped onion
- 2 tablespoons olive oil
- 2 teaspoons dried basil
- 1 teaspoon salt
- One teaspoon dried oregano

Instructions

Given below are the detailed instructions for cooking this tasty meal. You need to follow these instructions in the given order.

- Sauté peppers as well as onion in oil in a large saucepan until crisp-tender. Cook for an additional minute after adding the garlic. Drain the water.

- Add the tomato paste, water, tomato sauce, sugar, basil, salt, and oregano, and stir to combine.

- Bring the water to a boil. Reduce heat to low, cover, and cook for 30 minutes or until thoroughly heated.

- Meanwhile, grill sausages over medium heat, covered, for ten to sixteen minutes or when a thermometer registers 160°F, turning once or twice. It can be served on buns with cheese and sauce.

4. Teriyaki Portabella Mushroom Burger with Garlic Mayonnaise

Preparation time

30 minutes

Servings

2 persons

Ingredients

We have listed below the ingredients that are required for making this grilled food recipe:

- Two portabella mushrooms (around three and a half inches wide), cleaned with stems removed
- Two tablespoons bottled teriyaki sauce

- Two large (one to two ounces), thin slices of reduced-fat cheese
- Two whole-wheat hamburger buns
- Two leaves lettuce
- Four tomato slices
- One tablespoon light mayonnaise
- Half teaspoon minced garlic
- Quarter to half teaspoon lemon juice
- A few drops of Worcestershire sauce
- Add ground pepper and seasoning salt as per taste

Instructions

- Firstly, fire up the grill. Spread the teriyaki sauce over the mushrooms. Let them marinate while heating the coals.
- Grill the mushrooms 6 inches from the heat until they are soft (about 4-5 minutes a side).
- To melt, place cheese on top and grill briefly.
- Arrange burgers by placing on each bottom bun lettuce and tomato. Place the cheese-topped mushroom on top. Lightly spread on each top bun half the garlic mayonnaise and put on the mushroom top (the lettuce keeps the bottom bun from getting soggy).

5. Cajun Sirloin Burgers

Preparation time

50 minutes

Servings

4 persons

Ingredients

We have listed below the ingredients that are required for making this grilled food recipe:

- One-pound extra-lean ground beef
- Three tablespoons dry Italian breadcrumbs
- Three to four tablespoons egg substitute
- Three chopped green onions
- One tbsp Cajun seasoning
- One tbsp prepared mustard
- Four slices (about four ounces) reduced-fat cheese

- Four whole-grain buns

- Quarter cup barbecue sauce of your choice

- Four lettuce leaves

- Four large tomato slices

- Around twelve rings of red onion

Instructions

- Preheat the grill to a high level.

- Combine the ground beef, breadcrumbs, egg replacement, Cajun seasoning, green onions and mustard in an 8-cup measure by mixing with your fingertips. Shape into 4 patties, either with a patty press or by hand.

- Brush the grill grate lightly with canola cooking oil. Cook the patties on either side for 5 minutes or until well cooked. Place on each burger a slice of cheese and allow it to melt.

- Serve the burgers covered with lettuce, barbecue sauce, onion and tomato.

6. Grilled Eggplant and Pepper Goat Cheese Sandwiches

Preparation time

45 minutes

Servings

4 persons

Ingredients

We have listed below the ingredients that are required for making this grilled food recipe:

- One red bell pepper

- One eggplant, sliced lengthwise into quarter-inch slices

- Three tbsp low-fat bottled Italian

- You may also use balsamic vinaigrette

- Eight slices of whole-grain bread

- You may go for a French baguette cut lengthwise

- Two ounces soft goat cheese

- Quarter cup tapenade

Instructions

- Preheat the grill.

- Cut off the bell pepper's top; discard the rind and seeds. Get the pepper sliced into pieces.

Eggplant slices and bell pepper pieces are coated with low-fat bottled balsamic vinaigrette.

- On a grill covered with canola cooking spray, put the bell pepper pieces and eggplant slices. Grill till tender plus slightly browned (8-10 minutes), about 6 inches from the fire, turning after 4-5 minutes.

- Spread 4 bottom bread slices with goat cheese, then with tapenade. Cover with the slices of eggplant and a strip of red pepper the tapenade, then top with the remaining slices of bread.

- Cut each sandwich (if using whole-grain bread) into 2 or 4 triangles and eat.

7. Grilled Branzino with Preserved Lemon Gremolata

Preparation time

30 minutes

Servings

2 persons

Ingredients

We have listed below the ingredients that are required for making this grilled food recipe:

- One whole cleaned, gutted and de-scaled branzino

- One tbsp olive oil

- One tsp sea salt

- Half teaspoon pepper

- One lemon

- A little number of fresh herbs like rosemary, thyme, rosemary, parsley and sage

- One bunch of flat-leaf parsley. It should be finely chopped

- Quarter cup chopped preserved lemons

- Two finely chopped garlic cloves

- Half cup olive oil

- Cracked pepper

- Chili flakes

Instructions

- Make sure it's gutted and decaled when you buy a whole fish.

- Inside and out, rinse it off and pat it extra dry.

- Brush with oil freely.

- With salt and pepper, season generously, inside and out.

- Slice some lemons and place them within the fish cavity. Tuck in thyme, rosemary, sage or parsley.

- Cut 2-3 slits into either side of the fish at the thicker end using a sharp knife. The end of the tail can cook quicker than the end of the head, so this will allow the grill to cook evenly.

- Heat the grill to medium-high heat, 400F (or medium for more than 2 pounds of fish) and oil the grates. You may lower heat on one side, if necessary.

- Place the fish on a warm, greased grill with the end of the tail on the cooler side. For a 1 1/2-2-pound fish, or when you see grill marks, grill, wrapped, not moving it for approximately five minutes.

- Use a small metal spatula and tongs in order to flip carefully. Cover, grill until crisp, another 4-5 minutes, with clear grill marks.

- Create the flavorful Lemon Gremolata while grilling the fish, adding all the ingredients in a bowl and stirring.

- Place the fish on a platter and spoon the flavorful Gremolata on top right before serving.

- Enjoy this with Everyday Quinoa along with a leafy green salad.

8. Grilled Chicken Shawarma Recipe

Preparation time

30 minutes

Servings

6 persons

Ingredients

We have listed below the ingredients that are required for making this grilled food recipe:

- Two pounds to two and a quarter pounds chicken thighs

- Two tbsp ground cumin

- Two tbsp ground coriander

- Eight minced garlic cloves

- Two tsp kosher salt

- Six tbsp olive oil

- Quarter teaspoon cayenne pepper

- Two tsp turmeric

- One tsp ground ginger

- One tsp ground black pepper

- Two tsp all spice

Instructions

- Place all the marinade ingredients in a bowl and mix. You may also pulse to produce a paste in a food processor.

- Rub chicken with marinade on all sides and leave to rest for 20 minutes (or up to 24-48 hours refrigerated). Chicken can also be sliced into 1-inch cubes, and skewers can be made.

- On a preheated grill, grill chicken on medium-high heat, close the lid until good grill marks are on all sides, about 8 minutes per side. You can complete cooking in a 350 F oven or move to a cooler section of the grill until done, about 10 minutes, all the way through. (Alternatively, you should bake the thighs of chicken for 30-40 minutes in a 375 F oven)

- Enjoy the Shawarma of chicken with rice and vegetables or pita and tzatziki bread.

9. Thai Turkey Burgers with Crunchy Asian Slaw

Preparation time

45 minutes

Servings

3-4 persons

Ingredients

We have listed below the ingredients that are required for making this grilled food recipe:

Ingredients for Turkey Burger

- One pound ground turkey

- Three tbsp finely diced shallot. You may use red onion

- One and a half teaspoon fresh grated

- Two finely minced garlic cloves

- One tbsp finely chopped lemongrass

- Two tbsp chopped Thai basil

- One tsp lime zest

- One chopped scallion

- Half to one jalapeño

- One tbsp fish sauce

- One tsp sugar

- Quarter tsp white pepper

Ingredients for Crunchy Asian Slaw

- One cup of grated carrots
- One cup purple cabbage, shredded
- One thinly sliced scallion
- Two tbsp lime juice
- One tbsp olive oil
- One tsp sugar
- Quarter teaspoon salt & pepper

Ingredients for Spicy Aioli

- Quarter cup mayo or vegan mayo
- One to two tbsp sriracha

Instructions

- Preheat a medium-high grill.
- Combine all burger ingredients inside a medium bowl & use your hands to mix properly. Shape into one-inch 3 burgers with wet hands. Place it in the refrigerator on the plate.
- Toss the elements of the slaw together in a medium bowl.
- In a small bowl, combine the hot aioli ingredients altogether.
- Grill patties 4-5 minutes per side on an apre-heated, well-greased grill until golden & cooked through.
- Then Toast the buns or grill them.
- Spread the aioli on bottom bun. Then top with patty, the (optional) slaw, more aioli, cucumber ribbons, and finally, top bun.
- Enjoy.

10.Grilled Lamb Burger with Harissa Aioli

Preparation time

45 minutes

Servings

3 persons

Ingredients

We have listed below the ingredients that are required for making this grilled food recipe:

- Three fourth teaspoon kosher salt
- Half teaspoon cracked pepper
- Quick pickled onions
- crispy bacon
- Half cup mayo
- One to two tablespoons store-bought or homemade harissa paste
- One-pound organic ground lamb
- Two garlic cloves, finely minced
- Quarter cup very finely diced onion
- Half teaspoon smoked paprika
- Half teaspoon cumin
- Three brioche buns
- One cup baby arugula
- Three ounces Mahon cheese sliced

Instructions

- Heat grill to medium-high temperature.
- Prepare quick pickled onions.
- Mix ground lamb with onion, garlic, herbs, salt and pepper in a med bowl, using your hands, just to mix, being cautious not to over mix. Make patties, and set them aside.
- Crisp slices of bacon and set on a paper towel.
- Prepare the Harissa Aioli- whisking mayo in a small bowl with harissa paste or spices. Then set aside.
- Slice the cheese.
- Grill patties to medium or medium-rare when the grill is hot. Buns are to be toasted at the same

time.

- Top with cheese and close lid, turn off the heat and let the cheese melt— (or place in a warm oven, topping with cheese, to allow it to melt).

- Assemble. Assemble once the cheese has melted. On both sides of the buns, spread the harissa aioli, put the optional bacon, burgers, arugula and pickled onions. Finally, put the top of the bun. Immediately serve.

11. Grilled Naan with Garlic Scape Chutney

Preparation time

90 minutes

Servings

10 persons

Ingredients

We have listed below the ingredients that are required for making this grilled food recipe:

- One teaspoon sugar

- Half cup plain yogurt

- One large egg

- Quarter cup olive oil and more for brushing

- One and a half cup water

- Three fourth cup garlic scapes, chopped and tops removed (you can use cilantro or Italian parsley packed with 2 cloves of garlic)

- Five quarter cups of unbleached all-purpose flour; more as needed (optional: sub One cup whole wheat

- Three teaspoons baking powder

- One tbsp kosher salt

- Half teaspoon black pepper

- Half jalapeño or Serrano pepper- for a little kick (optional)

- One tbsp lime juice

- One third cup olive oil

- Half cup fresh mint packed

- Half cup roasted or smoked almonds

- Half teaspoons kosher salt

Instructions

- Make the dough: In the bowl of a stand mixer equipped with a dough handle, combine the flour, baking powder, salt and sugar. Whisk the yogurt and egg in a medium bowl and add 1-1/Two cups of lukewarm water and oil. Mix. Then pour the yogurt mixture into the flour mixture and blend for about 5 minutes, at low speed, until a soft, sticky dough begins to clump around the hook. Add more flour, 1 tsp, if the dough appears too wet.

- Line with parchment a baking sheet and dust gently with flour. Turn the dough out and divide it into 10 equal parts on a lightly floured surface. Make a ball of each piece and place them on the baking sheet. Brush the dough gently with oil, cover it with plastic and let it rest for 1 hour before shaping.

- Making the chutney: In a food processor, put all of the chutney ingredients and pulse until evenly granular.

- Roll a dough ball into a 5-inch circle on a lightly floured surface. In the middle, scatter 1 T of the chutney, leaving a 1/2-inch border. Sprinkle the chutney with one tablespoon of cheese. To form a pouch, gather the borders and pinch them to seal in the filling. Turn the pinched side of the pouch down and roll it into a 6-inch circle, using very light pressure. Move to a baking sheet that is parchment-lined. Layer, until ready to grill, a rolled-out naan with parchment.

- Prepare a medium charcoal or gas grill fire. Grill the bread pinched side down in batches, wrapped, until they puff up and gently brown the undersides in places, for 2 to 3 minutes. Next, turn over and cook the other side, wrapped, for 2 to 3 minutes, before the grill marks develop and the bread are cooked through. Turn the pinched bread side down and gently brush with butter or olive oil just before getting them off the grill. Serve it warm.

12. Sprouted Lentil Burgers (grill able and vegan)

Preparation time

24 hours 20 minutes

Servings

4 persons

Ingredients

We have listed below the ingredients that are required for making this grilled food recipe:

- One tbsp miso paste
- One tbsp olive oil
- Two tsp mustard, whole grain
- Two tsp granulated onion (or garlic)
- One tsp cumin

- One tbsp alternative sweetener or sugar

- Half tsp salt

- Optional addition- thinly sliced red onion or shallot, whole coriander, fennel seeds or cumin

- Half teaspoon coriander

- One and a half cup sprouted brown, green or black lentils

- One cup brown rice, cooked

- One cup lightly toasted walnuts-

- Half teaspoon salt

- Half teaspoon pepper

- Two to four tbsp tablespoons fresh herbs- scallions, cilantro parsley, basil, etc.

- Two to three tbsp toasted sesame seeds

- One raw beet, the size of a small tennis ball, peeled & grated

- Half cup vinegar, red wine

- Half cup water

Instructions

- Place one cup of whole lentils & 3 to 4 cups of water in a big mason jar in the morning and soak on the counter all day (or 8 hours).

- Drain well in the evening. Turn the jar on the side and let the lentils dry out a little, and let the lentils sit on the counter overnight. They are ready once you spot the little tip of white sprout starting to appear. Usually, it takes 24 to 30 hours.

- Put in the food processor one and a half cups of raw & sprouted lentils (properly drained), miso, cooked rice, oil, toasted walnuts, salt, mustard, garlic, spices and pepper and repeatedly pulse until well mixed & becomes a sturdy dough. Do not over process. You want it to be rough, not smooth. Otherwise, it could get pasty.

- Check one for the salt. If this tastes bland, make sure the miso has been correctly mixed in (also give some stir with the spoon, look for miso clump and pulse again).

- On a large plate or little sheet pan, place the piece of parchment. Sprinkle the sesame seeds on the parchment.

- Divide the dough into 4 balls with wet hands and shape 4 burgers, around one inch thick. Put on parchment and coat all sides with the sesame seeds.

- then Place inside the refrigerator uncovered while the grill is being heated (15 minutes- to firm up) (15 minutes- to firm up) (15 minutes- to firm up) (15 minutes- to firm up)

- They can also be pan-seared and done in a warm oven.

- Preheat the grill to med-high heat grill and the oven to almost 400 degrees F. The grill should be greased. Braise the lentil patties until they have a lot of grill marks on them, around 4 to 5 mins on either side, then put in the oven for 10 more minutes to finish warming all way through (or transfer to the cooler part of the grill) (Alternatively, go to a cooler portion of a grill)

- Make your burgers at this stage, or wrap & freeze to use later.

- Now, to make pickled beets, take sugar, liquids, salt and spices and bring them to simmer in a small pot. Add the onion and grated beets. Stir and cook for a couple of minutes before transferring to the fridge for chilling.

13. Grilled Pizza with Gorgonzola, Figs, Balsamic onions

Preparation time

40 minutes

Servings

4 persons

Ingredients

We have listed below the ingredients that are required for making this grilled food recipe:

- One pinch salt

- Eight figs- quartered

- handful arugula

- Two tbsp balsamic vinegar

- One pinch pepper

- One tsp sugar or honey

- Sixteen ounces pizza dough, divided into two balls

- One garlic clove- smashed

- One red onion- very thinly sliced into rings

- Two tbsp olive oil

- One cup grated Mozzarella

- One cup crumbled gorgonzola cheese

Instructions

- Heat oven to 450 F. You can also set the grill to high temperature.

- Let the dough rest for 20 minutes on a floured surface.

- Sauté the onion in oil over medium-high heat in a large skillet, constantly stirring for 3 minutes.

When the heat is low to mild, apply a pinch of salt. Continue to sauté for approximately 10 minutes before the onions start to caramelize and become tender. Add the balsamic, pepper and sugar. Continue to cook for another 3-4 minutes before the balsamic reduces. And put aside.

- Divide and spread the dough into 2 or 4 very thin rounds or ovals.
- Place directly on the hot grill while grilling, then grill for 2 to 3 minutes (until you get nice grill marks). Then flip and grill the other side. Put aside and repeat, or feel free to make more than one at a time if the grill is big enough.
- Rub each crust with crushed garlic, divide and scatter the cheese, top with figs and onions, or put them on top of a sheet pan in a hot oven to finish.

14. Healthy Burger Bowls

Preparation time

30 minutes

Servings

2 persons

Ingredients

We have listed below the ingredients that are required for making this grilled food recipe:

- Fresh vegetables- grated carrot, avocado, cucumber, grated beet, radish, tomatoes, shredded cabbage, sprouts, or whatsoever veggies you think of.
- Dressing- gorganzola, Caesar, balsamic, green goddess, tahini
- Burger patties (beef, lamb, turkey, chicken, vegan or veggie)
- grill-able vegetables- one onion, bell pepper, tomato, zucchini, eggplant, or asparagus
- Two large handfuls of fresh greens- spinach, arugula, mesclun, baby kale, or other types of salad greens

Instructions

- Preheat the grill to med-high heat.
- Prepare vegetables and burgers.
- Grill burgers along with veggies that can be grilled easily. Lower the heat after the appearance of grill marks.
- Assemble the bowls with veggies, greens, grilled veggies and burgers. Now spoon the dressing over the top. You may add the optional additions of your liking.

15. Lamb Kofta Lettuce Wraps

Preparation time

35 minutes

Servings

4-5 persons

Ingredients

We have listed below the ingredients that are required for making this grilled food recipe:

- Quarter cup packed Italian parsley –
- Quarter cup packed mint leaves- fresh
- One pound ground lamb
- One tsp kosher salt
- One tsp paprika (unsmoked)
- One tsp cumin
- Quarter cup toasted pine nuts
- A quarter of a medium red onion- rough chopped
- Two garlic cloves
- One tsp coriander
- Handful cherry tomatoes halved
- Tzatziki – store-bought or homemade
- Garnish with fresh mint, sprouts
- Half tsp ground allspice (it adds a good flavor-also do not leave this out)
- a generous pinch of alepo chili flakes- or regular, optional,
- leaves of Butter lettuce (or little gems, baby romaine)
- Two to three Turkish cucumbers, cut or sliced into thin spears

Instructions

- Preheat grill to medium-high temperature.
- In a food processor, put pine nuts, onion, fresh herbs and garlic and continuously pulse until finely ground, however not smooth.
- In a medium bowl, put the ground lamb with salt & all of the spices (cumin, allspice, paprika, chili flakes). Add to the bowl the herb pine nut mixture and blend well with wet palm, kneading to combine.

- Make sixteen 1 oz balls with wet hands. You may turn these into egg-like ovals and flatten them slightly or make circular balls and flatten them slightly. Place them on a pan.

- Clean and grease well when the grill is warm. Place on the grill the lamb koftas, change heat to med-high and cover it for 3 to 4 minutes. Use a metal spatula to flip. They can lose their grip on the grill while they develop grill marks. Switch heat to low after you flip all, cover & continue to cook until it is cooked through, approximately 5 minutes more- make sure to check 1 for doneness.

- Assembling the wraps: you may encourage guests to assemble these by themselves. You may pre-assemble wraps on a plate with butter lettuces, topped with tzatziki, tomato, and cucumber, and refrigerated while cooking kofta. Or only assemble while you cook.

- Top with the tzatziki, sprouts and torn leaves of mint.

CHAPTER 4: Grilled Chicken Recipes

Enjoy delicious cooking chicken on the grill for special occasions.

1. Grilled Sambal Chicken

Preparation time

30 minutes

Servings

4 persons

Ingredients

We have listed below the ingredients that are required for making this grilled food recipe:

- Quarter cup sriracha sauce
- Quarter cup fish sauce
- Half cup brown sugar
- Quarter cup vinegar, rice wine
- Quarter cup Sambal Olek

- Eight to ten Skewers, Pre-soaked

- Two and a half-pound Chicken

- Three garlic cloves

- One and a half tbsp sliced fresh Ginger

- Garnish Option: roasted crushed Peanuts, sliced scallions, fresh leaves of mint

- One eighth cup vegetable oil

- One tbsp Soy sauce or Bragg's Liquid Amino

Instructions

- Slice chicken into bite-sized pieces (to the skewer), or you can leave them whole and put them in the bowl or gallon zip-locked bag.

- Put in a blender the remainder of ingredients, except red chili paste (or Sambal Olek), and blend till smooth. To mix, whisk in the chili paste. Pour over chicken marinade & marinate for another 15 mins or overnight.

- Heat grill to medium-high heat.

- Skewer chicken (you can leave whole)

- In a small pot, pour the leftover marinade, bring to boil, and simmer for 5 to 10 minutes on low, until thickened & reduced. You're going to need it for basting the chicken.

- Place the chicken on greased, preheated, hot grill. Cover. Then Cook for 5 mins or longer before you see a deep grill mark. Switch over, baste, and cover. After both sides have a decent sear, and both the sides are well basted, turn the heat to very low or transfer to the upper rack & continue to cook through.

- Then Serve with the Thai Crunchy Salad. You can also garnish with scallions, fresh mint, and crushed salted peanuts.

2. Best Grilled Chicken Breast

Preparation time

45 minutes

Servings

4 persons

Ingredients

We have listed below the ingredients that are required for making this grilled food recipe:

- Two tablespoons brown sugar

- Three cloves garlic, minced

- Freshly ground black pepper
- Freshly chopped parsley for garnish
- One teaspoon dried thyme
- Quarter cup balsamic vinegar
- Three tablespoons extra-virgin olive oil
- One teaspoon dried rosemary
- Four chicken breasts
- Kosher salt

Instructions

- Mix together brown sugar, balsamic vinegar, olive oil, garlic and dried herbs in a bowl. Then season generously with salt and pepper.
- Now insert chicken into the bowl. Toss the ingredients to mix well. Allow it to marinate for a minimum of 20 minutes or overnight.
- Heat the grill to medium-high heat. Place chicken and grill, basting with marinade, till cooked through, at least 6 minutes each side.
- It can be garnished with parsley prior to serving.

3. Grilled chicken

Preparation time

1 hour 50 minutes

Servings

4-6 persons

Ingredients

We have listed below the ingredients that are required for making this grilled food recipe:

- Half to three fourth cup marinade
- Soy-Balsamic Marinade
- Wine and Herb Marinade
- Spiced Cider and Maple Marinade
- One-and-a-half-pound tender beef steaks; lamb or pork chops; skinned boned, chicken pieces; steaks or fish fillets, about one inch thick
- Pepper Lemon Marinade

Instructions

- The trim extra fat from the meat (as Flare-ups can be triggered by leaking fat.) Rinse pieces & pat dry; cut into small-size pieces if needed.

- put the meat inside a large zipper pouch. (one-gal. Size; look at notes). Seal the bag & turn to cover the pieces with marinade. Cool, occasionally turning, for meat and poultry for at least thirty mins or up to one day, and for fish for 20-30 minutes.

- Lift pieces with tongs & lay on grill 4-6 inches above a single, strong sheet of warm coals or extreme heat on heated gas grills (you can only hold the hand at the grill level for 2-3 seconds); close the gas lid. Discard the marinade.

- Halfway into cooking, flip the pieces with a large spatula or tongs. (For skin fish fillets, grilled skin side first down; to turn, slide a spatula underneath flesh & flip on the grill to another place. The skin should be removed and discarded.) You have to cook lamb or beef until it is done as you like, medium-rare 8-10 minutes in total; chicken and pork until they are not pink anymore in the middle of the thickest part, total 9-12 minutes. Move the meat to plate or dish and leave to rest for 2-3 mins before serving.

4. Easy Grilled Chicken Breast

Preparation time

20 minutes

Servings

4 persons

Ingredients

We have listed below the ingredients that are required for making this grilled food recipe:

- Three tbsp Worcestershire sauce

- Two tbsp. Dijon mustard

- One tbsp sugar

- One tsp garlic powder

- Four boneless skinless chicken breasts

- Two tbsp lemon juice

- Two tbsp Italian seasoning

- One third cup oil olive oil or vegetable oil

- Quarter cup cider vinegar (or red wine vinegar)

- One tbsp salt

- One tbsp pepper

Instructions

- Mix all marinade ingredients in a freezer bag or bowl. Then insert chicken and shake well to combine.

- Before initiating the cooking of chicken, you have to marinade it for at least 30 minutes (or up to 4 hours).

- Heat grill to medium-high heat.

- Put chicken on the grill for seven to eight minutes. Flip and cook for an additional seven to eight minutes or till no pink remains, and chicken touches 165°F.

- Let it sit for a maximum of five minutes before slicing.

5. Peruvian Chicken with Spicy Peruvian Green Sauce

Preparation time

40 minutes

Servings

4-6 persons

Ingredients

We have listed below the ingredients that are required for making this grilled food recipe:

- One and a half to two pounds chicken, either thigh or breast. Must be skinless and boneless

- Four finely minced garlic cloves

- Two tbsp olive oil

- Two tbsp lime juice

- Two tsp honey, agave or sugar

- One tbsp cumin

- Two tsp paprika. You may also use smoked paprika

- One tsp coriander

- One tsp dried oregano

- One tbsp fresh thyme

- One and a half teaspoon kosher salt

- One tsp soy sauce

- Half cup sour cream or mayo

- Half jalapeño

- One garlic clove

- One cup chopped cilantro. Go for thin stems

- Quarter teaspoon kosher salt

- One tablespoon lime juice

- Two cups diced and sliced cucumber

- One large and ripe avocado. Must be diced

- Yellow and red cherry tomatoes (a handful)

- Use cilantro leaves for garnishing

- Use olive oil for drizzling

- Five finger pinches of kosher salt

- One lime juice

Instructions

- **Preheat** the grill to medium temperature.

- If you are making rice, start it on the stove now.

- In a small bowl, prepare the marinade. Finely mince the garlic using a garlic press and put it in the bowl. Add honey, oil, lime juice, cumin, paprika, cilantro, salt and oregano and optional soy sauce. Then stir. Toss it in a bowl with the chicken, coat well on both sides, and/or brush it on the portobellos. For more flavor, you have to marinate until the grill heats up or overnight.

- By putting all the ingredients in a blender and blending until reasonably smooth, scraping down the sides if required, make Peruvian Green Sauce.

- Grill the chicken and/or portobellos while the grill is hot, sear all sides well, then turn down the heat or switch to a colder side of the grill to allow the chicken to cook.

- Make the salad in a large shallow bowl by putting it in the diced cucumber. Insert avocado, evenly spacing it out. Insert a pair of tomato cherry halves. Sprinkle with salt and pepper evenly and gently drizzle with the olive oil. With lime juice, add to the flavor. Garnish with leaves of cilantro.

- Serve with the Cilantro Lime Rice. Place 3/4 cups of rice on the bottom of the bowl; if making bowls, put sliced chicken or portobellos on one side, avocado salad on the other side, and drizzle with the cilantro sauce. Enjoy.

6. Sticky Barbecue Chicken

Preparation time

2 hours 55 minutes

Servings

8-10 persons

Ingredients

We have listed below the ingredients that would be required by you for cooking the healthy and tasty meal:

- Two tsp. garlic powder
- 2 Tbsp. unsulfured blackstrap molasses
- 1 Tbsp. Dijon mustard
- One Tbsp. Louisiana hot sauce
- 1 Tbsp. Worcestershire sauce
- One and a half tsp. cayenne pepper
- 12 skin-on, bone-in chicken thighs
- Zest and juice of 2 lemons
- 4 tsp. Diamond Crystals or 2.5 tsp. of Morton kosher salts
- 5 Tbsp. Barbecue Seasoning
- Barbecue Seasoning
- A quarter cup smoked paprika
- Two Tbsp. light brown sugar
- Two tsp. chili powder
- 1 Tablespoon vegetable oil, and extra for grill
- 1 small onion, finely chopped
- 3 garlic cloves, finely chopped
- 2 Tbsp. light brown sugar
- ¾ cup ketchup
- Two Tbsp. apple cider vinegar

Instructions

Given below are the detailed instructions for cooking this tasty meal. You need to follow these instructions in the given order.

- In a small mixing bowl, mix brown sugar, combine paprika, garlic powder, chili powder and cayenne. 12 cup (approximately).

- In a large mixing bowl, toss the chicken with the lemon juice and zest to coat. Toss with salt and 4 tablespoons seasoning and toss again to coat evenly. Allow a minimum of two hours and a maximum of twelve hours for chilling.

- In a medium saucepan, heat 1 tablespoon of oil over medium-high heat. Cook, occasionally stirring, until onion and garlic are tender, about 3 minutes. Cook, constantly stirring, for 2 minutes, or until brown sugar turns a shade darker. Add the remaining one tablespoon seasoning and cook, constantly stirring, for 30 seconds, or until fragrant. Cook, constantly stirring, until the ketchup has mildly darkened in color, approximately 2 minutes. In a large mixing bowl, combine the mustard, vinegar, molasses, hot sauce and Worcestershire sauce. Bring to a boil over high heat, constantly stirring for 2 minutes. Allow 5 minutes for cooling. Then you need to purée in a blender until completely smooth. Set aside the sauce.

- Then the grill is to be prepared for medium-high indirect heat (bank coals on one side of a charcoal grill; leave 1–2 burners off a gas grill). Grates should be lightly oiled. 5 minutes at direct heat, turning every minute, till chicken is browned on all sides. Transfer the chicken to indirect heat, cover, and grill, turning every five minutes or so until the chicken is cooked through. After 18–25 minutes, an instant-read thermometer placed inside the thickest part of the thighs registers 140°–145° F. Uncover grill and cook for another 10 minutes, basting **with reserved sauce as well as occasionally turning, till thermometer reads 165° F.**

7. Chicken Breasts with Romesco Sauce

Preparation time

1 hour 57 minutes

Servings

6 persons

Ingredients

We have listed below the ingredients that would be required by you for cooking the healthy and tasty meal:

- One teaspoon kosher salt

- 1 teaspoon smoked paprika

- ¾ teaspoon kosher salt

- A quarter teaspoon of cayenne pepper

- Lemon wedges for serving

- ½ teaspoon finely grated lemon zest

- ½ teaspoon dried oregano

- A quarter teaspoon freshly ground black pepper

- 4 boneless, skinless chicken breast halves, each (6 to 8 ounces)

- 2 medium red bell peppers

- 2 large garlic cloves

- A quarter cup extra-virgin olive oil

- A quarter cup fresh lemon juice

- 3 garlic cloves, minced or pushed through a press

- 1 teaspoon sweet paprika

- ¼ cup almonds, toasted

- A quarter cup extra-virgin olive oil

- 2 tablespoons tomato paste

- Two tablespoons sherry vinegar

Instructions

Given below are the detailed instructions for cooking this tasty meal. You need to follow these instructions in the given order.

- All marinade ingredients should be whisked together in a small bowl.

- Gently score the chicken breasts on the smooth (skin) side on the diagonal, making 3 or 4 evenly spaced (1/4 inch) deep slashes. Place the chicken in a mixing bowl, pour in the marinade, and toss to evenly coat. Cover the chicken with plastic wrap and chill for a minimum of one hour and a maximum of eight hours, turning it occasionally.

- Preheat the grill to medium-high heat-400° to 500°F- for direct cooking.

- Clean the cooking grates with a brush. The bell peppers are to be grilled at direct medium-high heat with the lid closed for about 20 minutes, turning every 5 minutes, until blackened all over. Place the peppers in a bowl with plastic wrap over them and steam for ten to fifteen minutes. Then take out the peppers from the bowl, peeling away the charred skin and discarding it, as well as the stems. Transfer the peppers to a food processor after coarsely chopping them. Combine the remaining sauce ingredients in a food processor and blend until smooth. Place in a mixing bowl.

- Preheat the grill to medium heat-350° to 450°F- for direct cooking.

- To avoid flare-ups, remove the chicken from the marinade and allow any excess marinade to drip back into the bowl. Remove the marinade and toss it out. Place the chicken on an angle to the grate bars, smooth (skin) side down, over direct medium heat. Grill for 4 to 6 minutes on the first side, with the lid closed, till the chicken breasts get good grill marks and easily release from the grates. Flip the chicken and cook for another 4 to 6 minutes, or unless an instant-read thermometer placed in the thickest part of the chicken registers 165°F. Then it is to be removed from the grill and set aside to rest for 3 to 5 minutes at room temperature indoors. Serve with lemon wedges and Romesco sauce.

8. Cuban Mojo Chicken Legs

Preparation time

5 hours 5 minutes

Servings

4 persons

Ingredients

We have listed below the ingredients that would be required by you for cooking the healthy and tasty meal:

- A half-cup fresh orange juice
- ½ teaspoon freshly ground black pepper
- 4 bone-in whole chicken legs, each
- Lime and orange wedges
- A quarter cup fresh lime juice
- ¼ cup olive oil
- Zest of one orange
- Zest of one lime
- 4 garlic cloves
- 1 small jalapeño pepper, seeded, coarsely chopped
- ½ cup packed cilantro leaves and tender stems
- 1 teaspoon ground cumin
- One teaspoon dried oregano
- 1½ teaspoon kosher salt

Instructions

Given below are the detailed instructions for cooking this tasty meal. You need to follow these instructions in the given order.

- Mix the marinade ingredients in the bowl of a food processor. Blend in the food processor.
- Place the chicken in a large re-sealable plastic bag, pour in the marinade, as well as seal the bag.

Then it is to be refrigerated for four to twenty-four hours, turning the bag occasionally to ensure even distribution of the marinade.

- Over medium heat (350° to 450°F), start preparing the grill for indirect as well as direct cooking.

- Remove the chicken from the marinade, reserving any excess liquid in the bag. Fill a small saucepan halfway with the marinade. Bring to a boil over medium heat, then reduce to low heat and cook for 2 minutes. Then it should be cooled to room temperature after removing from the heat.

- Grill the chicken skin-side up for 40 minutes at indirect medium heat with the lid closed, then switch to direct medium heat. Continue to grill, lid closed, for another 8 to 10 minutes, or unless an instant-read thermometer placed inside the thickest part of the chicken reads 165°F as well as the chicken is well marked. Remove from the grill and set aside to rest for 3 to 5 minutes at room temperature indoors

9. Buttermilk Brined Rotisserie Chicken

Preparation time

1 hour 50 minutes

Servings

4-6 persons

Ingredients

We have listed below the ingredients that would be required by you for cooking the healthy and tasty meal:

- 2 tablespoons sugar
- Thyme sprigs, for garnish
- Lemon wedges, for garnish
- 1 tablespoon fresh thyme leaves
- 2 teaspoons finely grated lemon zest
- 1½ quart buttermilk
- ¼ cup kosher salt
- 6 cloves garlic, minced or pushed through a press
- 1 teaspoon freshly ground black pepper
- One whole chicken

Instructions

Given below are the detailed instructions for cooking this tasty meal. You need to follow these instructions in the given order.

- To dissolve the salt and sugar, whisk together all of the brine ingredients in a bowl that is big enough to hold the chicken.

- Refrigerate the chicken, breast side down, in the brine for eight to twenty-four hours, turning occasionally.

- Take the chicken from the brine when ready to grill, allowing any excess liquid to drip back into the bowl. Remove the brine and discard it. Using paper towels, pat the chicken dry on the inside and out. Secure the legs and wings of the chicken with butcher's twine.

- Using the spit forks, secure the trussed chicken on the rotisserie spit.

- Place the spit on the grill as well as turn on the motor prior to actually turning on the grill to ensure that your food fits and spins freely on the rotisserie.

- Over medium heat-350° to 450°F- start preparing the grill for indirect cooking.

- Place the spit on the grill, turn on the motor, and position the drip pan underneath the chicken.

- Now the chicken is to be removed from the spit and remove from the grill. Allow for five to ten minutes of resting time indoors at room temperature before carving. Cut the trussing into serving pieces and discard the trussing. It can be served with lemon wedges and fresh thyme as a garnish.

10. Chicken Drumsticks with Barbecue Sauce

Preparation time

1 hour 30 minutes

Servings

8 persons

Ingredients

We have listed below the ingredients that would be required by you for cooking the healthy and tasty meal:

- 1 teaspoon dried oregano

- One and a half teaspoon granulated onion

- 16 chicken drumsticks

- ¾ cup barbecue sauce

- 1 teaspoon ground black pepper

- 1 teaspoon chili powder

- 2 tablespoons sweet paprika

- 1 tablespoon fine sea salt

- 1 tablespoon brown sugar

- One and a half teaspoon granulated garlic

Instructions

Given below are the detailed instructions for cooking this tasty meal. You need to follow these instructions in the given order.

- Combine all of the rub ingredients in a small bowl and stir well.

- Hold a drumstick by the bone and cut around the bony end with a small, sharp knife, cutting through the skin, meat as well as sinews. The sinews, skin and cartilage at the base of the drumstick should be pulled or cut away. Cut the joint at the base with kitchen scissors. To make the drumstick look like a lollipop, push the meat toward the top end. Using a paper towel, wipe away any remaining residue from the bone. Repeat with the rest of the drumsticks.

- Each chicken lollipop should be evenly coated in the rub.

- Preheat the grill to medium-low heat-250° to 350°F- for indirect cooking. Clean the cooking grates with a brush. Place the ETC system on the grates, along with the expansion rack.

- Place the chicken lollipops in the rack with the meat facing up. Alternatively, each lollipop can be threaded onto a metal skewer. Grill the lollipops for about 15 minutes at indirect medium-low heat with the lid closed. Brush some of the barbecue sauce on the lollipops, close the lid, as well a grill for fifteen minutes. Brush and grill for a total of two more times. They're done when an instant-read thermometer placed inside the thickest part of the chicken (but not touching the bone) reads 165°F, which takes about 1 hour. The barbecue sauce gives them a nice reddish color. Serve right away.

CHAPTER 5: Grilled Salads Recipes

Enjoy making delicious salads on the grill for special occasions.

1. Grilled Corn

Preparation time

27 minutes

Servings

4-8 persons

Ingredients

We have listed below the ingredients that are required for making this grilled food recipe:

- Four to eight ears of fresh corn
- Butter, sea salt, lemon or lime wedges, red pepper flakes
- Vegan Ranch
- Cilantro Lime Butter

Instructions

- Pull back the corn husks, leaving them connected to the base. Remove the silks and close the husks back over the corn cob (as much as you can). Soak the corn for 10 minutes in a big pot of cold water. This will avoid the burning of too many husks on the grill. Drain and pat it to dry.

- Heat the grill to medium heat. Place the corn on the grill and cook for about 15 minutes, rotating every three to five minutes, till all sides of the corn are cooked. Remove it from the grill. Then tie the husks back and use them like a stick. Serve with toppings of your choice.

2. Grilled Romaine Salad with Corn, Fava Beans and Avocado

Preparation time

35 minutes

Servings

4 persons

Ingredients

We have listed below the ingredients that are required for making this grilled food recipe:

- Two romaine hearts, sliced in half lengthwise
- Olive oil for brushing (You can also use olive oil spray)
- One shucked ear corn
- Half pound fresh fava beans in pods
- One lemon sliced in half
- Half pound peeled, raw and deveined shrimp
- One diced avocado
- One-pint cherry or grape tomatoes, sliced in half.
- Fresh herbs such as Italian parsley or dill

Ingredients for yogurt dill dressing

- Half cup plain yogurt
- One tbsp olive oil
- One tbsp lemon juice
- One finely minced fat clove garlic
- Two tbsp chopped dill
- Quarter teaspoon salt and pepper as per taste

Ingredients for a lemon dressing

- Four tbsp olive oil

- One tbsp sherry vinegar

- One tbsp lemon juice

- One tsp honey or agave

- One tsp sumac

- Half teaspoon salt

- One minced fat garlic clove

Instructions

- Heat grill to medium-high.

- Whisk together the dressing ingredients and set them aside.

- Brush or spray Romaine with olive oil and season with salt, then briefly grill each side (leave the lid open) till nice grill marks show, but not so long that the crunch of the lettuce is lost. Set these on a large cutting board, platter, or sheet pan.

- Grill the lemon over medium heat (cut-side should be down), fava beans, corn on the cob and optional shrimp. Once the fava beans are tender, shuck and divide between the Romaine wedges for about 10 minutes. Cut off the corn from the kernels and divide. Add the sliced avocado and the halved cherry tomatoes. Add it now if you're using shrimp. Squeeze the grilled lemon halves into the salad, then spoon over the top with a little dressing. Scatter it with fresh herbs.

3. Grilled Romaine Salad with Maitake Mushrooms

Preparation time

20 minutes

Servings

2 persons

Ingredients

We have listed below the ingredients that are required for making this grilled food recipe:

- One large Maitake Mushroom (Should be the size of a large orange)

- Two tbsp olive oil or butter or use both in combination

- One smashed garlic clove

- Use salt and pepper as per taste

- One large head of romaine lettuce

- Garnish with capers, chives

- Use furikake seasoning for sprinkling

- Quarter cup mayo

- One tbsp rice wine vinegar

- Two tsp anchovy paste

- Half teaspoon finely minced or grated fresh ginger

- One finely minced or grated fat garlic clove

- Quarter teaspoon salt

- Use pepper as per taste

- Half teaspoon furikake seasoning

Instructions

- Heat grill to medium-high.

- Cut the Maitake mushroom halfway to the end of the stem. Slice each half into thick slices of one-third of an inch. There are 6-8 slices you can have. Over medium melt, heat the oil or butter in a skillet. Season the oil thoroughly with salt and pepper and apply the crushed clove of garlic, stirring until fragrant for around 2 minutes. Get the garlic removed.

- Pan sear until golden, soft and slightly crispy on either side of the mushroom. Each side for about 4-5 minutes. Just put it aside.

- Make the dressing: Mash them with garlic and ginger with a mortar and pestil when using whole anchovies. In a small bowl, combine with the remaining ingredients.

- Suppose Anchovy paste is being used, then whisk-mayo, vinegar, and anchovy paste until they are smooth. Ginger, garlic, salt and a few twists of cracked pepper are added. Stir in optional seasoning for furikake and set aside.

- Cut the romaine lettuce in half when the grill is hot. Brush with the olive oil on the cut side of the romaine. On the grill, put the cut side down and sear, leaving the lid open. Just sear before grill marks surface, about 2 minutes. In Romaine, you want to leave the crispness, but don't overdo it or let it collapse. Take it off the grill and put it on two plates.

- Divide the mushrooms of the pan-seared Maitake and put on top of each half of the grilled Romaine. Over the Romaine and mushrooms, spoon the dressing. Sprinkle with the furikake seasoning and a few capers.

- Scatter with some fresh chives.

- Serve quickly with a knife and fork and devour.

4. Chipotle Grilled Chicken Salad with Grilled Corn, Peppers and Quinoa

Preparation time

45 minutes

Servings

2 persons

Ingredients

We have listed below the ingredients that are required for making this grilled food recipe:

- Two pieces of Mexican Grilled Chipotle Chicken
- One shucked ear corn
- One halved and seeded red bell pepper
- Four to six whole scallions
- Olive oil for brushing
- One and a half cup of cooked quinoa
- Two to three cups arugula
- One sliced avocado
- Little quantity of halved cherry tomatoes
- Quarter cup cilantro leaves
- Use salt and pepper as per taste
- Four tbsp olive oil
- Two tbsp lime juice
- One tbsp honey or agave
- Half teaspoon salt
- Half teaspoon coriander
- Quarter to half teaspoon ground chipotle powder. You can add more as per taste

Instructions

- Heat grill to medium-high.
- Grill the chicken.
- Brush with olive oil (or use olive oil spray) scallion, the red bell pepper halves and an ear of corn and grill until tender and grill marks emerge, around 5-8 minutes.
- Cut off the corn kernels, slice the avocado, slice the bell pepper and slice the cherry tomatoes

in two.

- If you are using chicken, then slice the chicken.

- Create the dressing by whisking them all in a little bowl together.

- Assemble the bowls. Divide the quinoa and arugula and layer them, then place the grilled chicken around the bowl with grilled peppers, grilled corn, sliced avocado and tomatoes.

- Sprinkle a little salt and pepper (particularly avocado, corn and tomatoes.)

- Cover with some of the other garnishes you need and cilantro.

- Spoon the dressing of Chipotle Lime over the top (you may not need it all).

- Enjoy these or pack them up immediately for a tasty takeaway lunch on the go.

5. Summer Nicoise Salad with Grilled Fish

Preparation time

40 minutes

Servings

6 persons

Ingredients

We have listed below the ingredients that are required for making this grilled food recipe:

- One teaspoon kosher salt

- One ground pepper

- zest of one lemon

- A quarter cup of olive oil

- Four finely minced cloves of garlic

- Four to six fish boneless, skinless fillets

- One tbsp mustard, whole grain

Salad ingredients

- Half cup sliced roasted red bell pepper

- Greens, spinach or arugula for 4-6 people, approx. 1 lb.

- Eight ounces cherry tomatoes

- Half pound green beans blanched and trimmed

- Quarter cup niçoise or kalamata olives sliced

- Fifteen ounces canned cannellini beans washed & drained (or one and a half cup cooked) or three boiled eggs, sliced in half

- Ten new baby potatoes halved & blanched

- Two tablespoons capers, drained.

Nicoise Dressing Ingredients

- One tablespoon fresh thyme leaves or oregano

- Half cup chopped Italian parsley

- Quarter cup lemon juice & zest of 1 lemon (the Meyer Lemon's great)

- One tbsp vinegar, red wine

- Three fourth teaspoon Kosher Salt

- black pepper, fresh ground

- Half cup olive oil, extra-virgin

- Half cup finely diced red onion

- Two tsp mustard whole grain

Instructions

- First, Mix all fish marinade ingredients in a medium-sized bowl & coat on the fish, marinating for a minimum of half an hour or, ideally, overnight.

- Boil green beans and white potatoes. When cooled, put it aside.

- Preheat the grill to a medium temperature.

- Prepare Nicoise dressing. In a medium bowl, combine all the ingredients together. To the dressing, add the roasted peppers, cannellini beans, capers and olives, and let marinate.

- Now Grill the fish over a med-high grill, & flip thoroughly after 5 minutes with a metal spatula, and if possible, low heat or transfer to a chiller spot-or put on foil. You can also put on a layer of lemon pieces until cooked appropriately. Put aside and lightly cover with foil.

- Prepare the salad. Place a nice bed of green veggies onto an extra-large dish. To coat the greens, scoop some Nicoise dressings from the cup and half of the marinated veggies over greens.

- Now Arrange the green beans and potatoes and top them with the charred fish. Then garnish with slices of cherry tomatoes & remaining spoon dressings (depending upon the size of dressing-you might not want all) and finish with peppers/white beans over the top.

- Then Give the fish little cracked pepper and lemon squeeze to taste.

6. Mango & Grilled Chicken Salad

Preparation time

25 minutes

Servings

4 persons

Ingredients

We have listed below the ingredients that would be required by you for cooking the healthy and tasty meal:

- 1 pound of chicken tenderloins
- A half teaspoon salt
- A quarter tsp pepper
- six cups salad greens, torn mixed
- A quarter cup balsamic or raspberry vinaigrette
- one medium-sized mango, peeled & cubed
- One cup sugary snap peas, fresh, halved lengthwise

Instructions

Given below are the detailed instructions for cooking this tasty meal. You need to follow these instructions in the given order.

- Season the chicken with pepper and salt before serving. Wet the paper towels with the cooking oil and rub them on the grill rack with long-handled tongs to lightly coat them. Grill the chicken, covered, at medium heat for 3-4 minutes on each side until it isn't any longer pink. Chicken should be cut into 1-inch pieces.
- Drizzle vinaigrette over greens and divide among 4 plates. Serve immediately with mango, chicken, and peas on top. round chicken tender

CHAPTER 6: Grilled Seafood Recipes

Enjoy cooking delicious seafood on the grill for special occasions.

1. Grilled Salmon Tzatziki Bowl

Preparation time

30 minutes

Servings

2 persons

Ingredients

We have listed below the ingredients that are required for making this grilled food recipe:

- Eight to ten ounces of salmon
- Olive oil for brushing
- Add salt and pepper as per taste
- Juice of one lemon

Instructions

- Heat grill to medium-high.
- Set up one cup of quinoa or rice to cook on the stove. (Quinoa would take 15-20 minutes only)
- Brush the olive oil on the salmon and season with salt and pepper. And put aside.

- Make or use the store-bought Tzatziki sauce.

- Along with some other veggies you want to grill, put salmon on the grill (brush with olive oil, salt and pepper). Grill the salmon on both sides for three to four minutes, depending on the thickness of the cut. Grill the lemon with an open side down till strong grill marks emerge. (Before eating, you can use the grilled lemon and squeeze over the salmon.)

- Assemble the 2 bowls when the veggies and salmon are done.

- Divide the quinoa into 2 bowls. Put a handful of greens on top. Drizzle with a little olive oil. Then sprinkle with salt after adding some fresh vegetables you want. Arrange the salmon and grilled vegetables on top. Over the whole bowl, squeeze the grilled lemon. Put few generous tzatziki sauce spoonfuls over the top of the salmon. Serve with herbs.

2. Pineapple chipotle shrimp skewers

Preparation time

30 minutes

Servings

3-4 persons

Nutritional facts

378 calories

Ingredients

We have listed below the ingredients that are required for making this grilled food recipe:

- One lime – One eighth cup lime juice and its zest

- One orange- Quarter cup orange juice

- Half teaspoon chipotle powder, more for spicy (or Half of a canned chipotle chili in adobo sauce)

- Garnish – limes, cilantro, Jicama Mango Slaw

- One tbsp honey or maple

- Three cloves roughly chopped garlic

- One pound big raw, deveined and peeled shrimp (16 to 20 or 21 to 15 size)

- One pound of pineapple chunks- slice to the exact same thickness as shrimp (approximately ¾" thick)

- Three tbsp olive oil

- One tsp salt

- Half teaspoon cumin

- Half teaspoon coriander
- Half tsp chili powder

Instructions

- When using wood, soak the skewers.
- Place the shrimp in a ziplock bag or bowl.
- In a mixer, blend the marinade ingredients all together until smooth.
- Then Pour over the shrimp into the marinade and marinate for 30 mins or even overnight. Then pineapple is to be prepared.
- Preheat the grill to med-high temperature.
- Drain marinade into a shallow saucepan from the bowl or bag.
- Skewer shrimp & pineapple alternating onto skewers (Skewer the pineapple in a horizontal way so that shrimp & pineapple are around the same distance and all lie flat on the grill. You'll get a nice grill mark on all of them that way. This must make skewers of 10 to 12 x ten inches.
- Give marinade a short simmer till it darkens and thickens a little. Turn off the heat.
- Grease grill well.
- Then Lay down the skewers, grill each side for about three minutes till great grill marks are formed and shrimp is properly cooked. But do not overcook shrimp.
- Put on a serving platter. Sprinkle with marinade or some lime.
- Immediately serve.

3. Grilled Salmon with Pickled Huckleberry Relish

Preparation time

30 minutes

Servings

4 persons

Ingredients

We have listed below the ingredients that are required for making this grilled food recipe:

- Half cup applewood chips
- Thyme
- Quarter teaspoon salt
- One teaspoon whole coriander seeds
- One large shallot- finely minced

- lemon zest and juice

- One and a half cup fresh huckleberries

- One and a half to two pounds Fillet of Wild Salmon (skin on)

- Olive oil for brushing and salt and pepper

- Half cup sugar (or honey)

- Half cup red wine vinegar

Instructions

- Heat grill to medium-high.   Make a small bowl the size of half a grapefruit out of 2-3 layers of foil. Within the foil bowl, place applewood chips, place them directly on the heating grill and close the grill lid.

- Make Relish: In a medium bowl, put huckleberries. In a small saucepan, heat the sugar (or honey), vinegar, salt, and coriander seeds, and whisk until the sugar is dissolved. Add the minced shallots. Then simmer for two minutes. Pour over the hot liquid on huckleberries, whisk and set aside. This can be prepared in advance and refrigerated overnight or used immediately.

- Brush the salmon with olive oil on both sides and sprinkle with salt and pepper. Switch heat down to low once applewood chips start smoking, grill salmon, skin side down, directly on the grill, at the lowest heat, and sprinkle with one lemon zest and one tablespoon thyme leaves. The lid should be closed.

- After 5 minutes, check. Move the salmon to create crosshatch marks on its skin. Then close the lid again for a few minutes. Salmon will cook quickly at this stage, especially if it's a thinner slice.

- Turn off the heat once the salmon is cooked to medium-rare or medium.

- Use two extra-large spatulas to carefully put salmon over greens on a plate. Squeeze half a lemon. The pickled huckleberry relish, along with a little pickling liquid, is generously spooned over the salmon and greens. Then scatter with thyme sprigs. Immediately serve.

4. Cedar Planked Salmon with Lemon Butter

Preparation time

50 minutes

Servings

4 persons

Ingredients

We have listed below the ingredients that would be required by you for cooking the healthy and tasty meal:

- A quarter teaspoon black pepper, freshly ground

- 1 center-cut skin-on salmon fillet, (1.5-2 pounds) and (¾-1¼") thick, the pin bones to be removed
- 1 thinly sliced lemon, seeded
- 2 tablespoons extra-virgin olive oil
- 2 teaspoons light brown sugar
- 1 teaspoon kosher salt
- four tablespoons softened unsalted butter,
- one tablespoon dill, finely chopped
- 1 teaspoon lemon zest, finely grated
- ½ tsp kosher salt
- A half teaspoon lemon zest, finely grated
- A half teaspoon black pepper, freshly ground

Instructions

Given below are the detailed instructions for cooking this tasty meal. You need to follow these instructions in the given order.

- In a small mixing bowl, mix all of the butter ingredients as well as mash well with a fork.
- Submerge the cedar plank in a baking dish full of water. Soak the plank for a minimum of 1 hour after weighing it down with the cans.
- Combine all of the oil ingredients in a small bowl.
- Place salmon on the work surface, skin side down. Cut the salmon into four serving pieces without piercing skin. Brush approximately seventy percent of oil onto salmon flesh.
- Preheat the grill to med-high heat about 400-500° F- for direct cooking.
- Close the lid and place the plank over the direct heat. After three to ten mins, use the long-handle tongs for turning the plank over when it begins to smoke and toast. Place the salmon skin-side down on the plank's toasted side. Place the lemon slices on top of the salmon and brush them lightly with the remaining oil.
- With the lid closed, grill the salmon over the direct med-high heat till a thermometer (instant-read) placed inside the thicker part of salmon reads 125°-130° F.
- Move fillet on a plank to the heatproof surface before serving. Remove the skins from the portions as well as serve with lemons and lemon butter pads.

5. Grilled Oysters with Pecorino and Shaved Bottarga

Preparation time

30 minutes

Servings

8-10 persons

Ingredients

We have listed below the ingredients that would be required by you for cooking the healthy and tasty meal:

- 1 1/2 teaspoon minced garlic
- Two dozen large oysters, like Gulf or bluepoint
- Aged Pecorrino Romano & mullet bottargas, for serving
- 1 1/2 tsp. minced thyme leaves
- 2 sticks unsalted butter, softened
- 2 tbsp. fresh lemon juice
- Kosher salt and freshly ground black pepper

Instructions

Given below are the detailed instructions for cooking this tasty meal. You need to follow these instructions in the given order.

- Preheat the grill. Season the butter, thyme, lemon juice and garlic with salt & pepper in a large mixing bowl. Shuck oysters, leaving the meat as well as juices in concave shell, & top each with a teaspoon of compound butter.
- Place oyster halves onto the grill. Ensure that the shell side is down, & cook for about 5 minutes, or till the juices start to bubble as well as oyster meat starts to curl from the edges. Transfer the oysters to a serving platter after removing them from the grill.

6. Grilled Caesar Salmon Foil Packets

Preparation time

25 minutes

Servings

2 persons

Ingredients

We have listed below the ingredients that would be required by you for cooking the healthy and tasty meal:

- 6 small sweet peppers sliced
- 1 tablespoon olive oil
- 2 tablespoons creamy Caesar dressing
- 2 lemons sliced
- 6 grilled artichoke heart jarred
- salt and pepper to taste
- 2 sheets Reynolds Wrap foil
- 2 6-ounce Salmon Filets
- Two tomatoes cut into wedges
- 1 tablespoon fresh lemon juice

Instructions

Given below are the detailed instructions for cooking this tasty meal. You need to follow these instructions in the given order.

- Preheat the grill to 450 degrees Fahrenheit.
- Fold both sheets of foil in half on a large tray, leaving one side open.
- On 1 side of each piece of foil, place the salmon in the center.
- Vegetables should be placed on each piece of salmon.
- You have to season to taste with salt and pepper.
- To each of the salmon filet, squeeze half tbsp of fresh lemon juice.
- Drizzle 1/2 tablespoon olive oil over each salmon as well as the veggie group.
- One tablespoon Caesar dressing brushed on each salmon filet
- Each salmon filet should have three lemon pieces on it.
- To make the foil packets, fold down the top piece of foil as well as cinch up the sides.

- Place the salmon on the grill for fifteen minutes or until it is fully cooked.

7. Lemony Shrimp & Tomatoes

Preparation time

25 minutes

Servings

2 persons

Ingredients

We have listed below the ingredients that would be required by you for cooking the healthy and tasty meal:

- 1-pound uncooked jumbo shrimp, peeled and deveined
- A half teaspoon of sugar
- 1/2 teaspoon salt, divided
- 12 cherry tomatoes
- 1/4 teaspoon pepper
- 2/3 cup fresh arugula
- 2 green onions, sliced
- 1/4 cup plain yogurt
- 2 teaspoons 2% milk
- 1/3 cup lemon juice
- 2 tablespoons olive oil
- 2 garlic cloves, minced
- A half teaspoon grated lemon zest
- 1 teaspoon cider vinegar
- 1 teaspoon Dijon mustard

Instructions

Given below are the detailed instructions for cooking this tasty meal. You need to follow these instructions in the given order.

- Whisk together the lemon juice, oil, garlic, and lemon zest in a large mixing bowl until well combined. Toss in the shrimp to coat. Allow for a 10-minute rest period.
- In a food processor, combine mustard, milk, arugula, green onions, yogurt, vinegar, sugar, and 1/4 teaspoon salt; process until smooth.

- Thread shrimp as well as tomatoes alternately on four metal skewers. Now you have to season with the remaining salt and pepper.
- Grill for 2-3 minutes on each side over medium-high heat till shrimp are no longer pink. Serve with a side of sauce.

8. Garlic Butter Salmon

Preparation time

25 minutes

Servings

4 persons

Ingredients

We have listed below the ingredients that would be required by you for cooking the healthy and tasty meal:

- 1 tablespoon finely minced fresh rosemary
- I Can't Believe It's Not Butter! Original Spray
- 4 salmon fillets 6 ounces each
- 1 teaspoon coarse sea salt
- 1 tablespoon minced garlic about 2 cloves
- 1/2 lemon juiced (about 1 tablespoon)
- A half teaspoon of pepper

Instructions

Given below are the detailed instructions for cooking this tasty meal. You need to follow these instructions in the given order.

- Preheat the grill and liberally spray a grill pan.
- Mix the rosemary, garlic, lemon juice, salt, and pepper in a small bowl.
- Then the garlic paste is to be spread over each piece of salmon.
- Remove the salmon from the refrigerator and spray it four times.
- Spray the bottom of each piece of salmon and flip it over, so the skin side is up on the grill pan.
- Cover and cook for 4-5 minutes before flipping each salmon filet.
- Remove the salmon from the grill when it is fully cooked and serve.

9. Easy Grilled Sesame Salmon

Preparation time

25 minutes

Servings

4 persons

Ingredients

We have listed below the ingredients that would be required by you for cooking the healthy and tasty meal:

- 1 tbsp. Toasted Sesame
- Salt & Pepper
- 2 tsp Olive Oil
- 1 tsp. Cumin
- 1/2 Salmon Filet
- 1/2 cup Pistachios, crushed
- 1 tsp. Coriander
- One Lemon, Zested

Instructions

Given below are the detailed instructions for cooking this tasty meal. You need to follow these instructions in the given order.

- Preheat your grill to 300 degrees F and prepare it for indirect heat.
- Over a baking sheet, put a greased cooling rack. Remove the salmon from the package, rinse if necessary, and pat dry thoroughly. If necessary, remove any pin bones.
- Pulse the pistachios in a food processor to make them finer.
- Combine all of the remaining ingredients, including the pistachios, in a mixing bowl and stir until well combined.
- Coat the salmon flesh lightly with olive oil, then apply a thin, even layer over the top.
- Cook the baking sheet indirectly on the cooler side of the grill till the thickest part attains 425 degrees F.

10. Easy Grilled Sesame Shrimp with Shishito Peppers

Preparation time

20 minutes

Servings

8-12 persons

Ingredients

We have listed below the ingredients that would be required by you for cooking the healthy and tasty meal:

- One tsp Salt & Pepper, divided
- 1-2 tsp. Toasted Sesame Seeds
- Two tbsp. Sesame Oil, divided
- 2 tbsp Chili Paste or Sauce
- 1 tbsp. Soy Sauce or Coconut Aminos
- 1 lb. Peeled & Deveined Shrimp
- 6 oz. Shishito Peppers
- 1 Lemon or Lime, juiced

Instructions

Given below are the detailed instructions for cooking this tasty meal. You need to follow these instructions in the given order.

- Set aside the shishito peppers with the remaining sesame salt, oil and pepper until you're ready to prepare the shrimp.
- Using skewers, skewer the shrimp and peppers. Thread each shrimp evenly onto both skewers, spacing them no more than an inch apart. It'll be easier to turn and grill as a result of this. Carry out the same procedure with your peppers.
- Heat the grill to medium-high and cook the shrimp and peppers for a minute or two on each side. The shrimp should be cooked to a temperature of 145 degrees Fahrenheit, and the peppers must have mildly blistered skin all around.
- Remove the skewers and remove the meat from the grill. It can be served with a dipping sauce or over cauliflower rice.

11. Grilled Shrimp with Oregano and Lemon

Preparation time

1hour 30 minutes

Servings

8 persons

Ingredients

We have listed below the ingredients that would be required by you for cooking the healthy and tasty meal:

- 1 minced garlic clove,
- pepper, Freshly ground
- 2.5 pounds of large shrimps, shelled & deveined
- some Salt
- ¾ cup olive oil, extra-virgin
- 1 teaspoon lemon zest, finely grated
- 1/2 cup of salted capers—washed, soaked for one hour & drained
- 1/2 cup of oregano leaves
- 3 tablespoons lemon juice, freshly squeezed

Instructions

Given below are the detailed instructions for cooking this tasty meal. You need to follow these instructions in the given order.

- Thinly slice drained capers, oregano leaves, & garlic on a cutting board. Carefully transfer to a mixing bowl and add a half-cup & 2 tablespoons olive oil, as well as the lemon juice and zest. Season sauce with a pinch of black pepper.

- Preheat the grill. Toss shrimps with the remaining two tbsp of the olive oil in a large mixing bowl, as well as season gently with salt & pepper. Thread shrimp onto metal skewers as well as grill over the high heat, flipping once, for 3 minutes per side, or until lightly charred & cooked through. Transfer the shrimp to a platter after removing them from skewers. Serve with a dollop of sauce on the top.

12. Citrus-Soy Squid

Preparation time

45 minutes

Servings

4 persons

Ingredients

We have listed below the ingredients that would be required by you for cooking the healthy and tasty meal:

- One cup mirin
- 1 cup soy sauce
- 1/3 cup yuzu juice or fresh lemon juice
- Two cups water
- 2 pounds squid tentacles left whole; bodies cut crosswise 1 inch thick

Instructions

Given below are the detailed instructions for cooking this tasty meal. You need to follow these instructions in the given order.

- Mix the yuzu juice, mirin, soy sauce and water in a mixing bowl.
- Refrigerate half of the marinade in an airtight container for later use. Add the squid to the bowl with the leftover marinade and set aside for at least 30 minutes or up to 4 hours at room temperature.
- Preheat the grill. The squid should be drained. Grill for 3 minutes at moderately high heat, flipping once, till tender and white throughout. Serve immediately.

Conclusion

Grilling is the closest thing to cooking over an open fire. Grilling is the process of cooking food by skewering it onto skewers attached to hot, glistening coal. Grilling can also be done by placing food steaks on a grilling pan with ridges so that the juices of the food are separated, and the food is almost completely cooked. Food that is grilled is the way to go. There are a few distinct advantages, both in terms of health and flavor. Grilling requires less fat, perhaps just a light coating before placing it under the grill to help the cooking process get started. As fat drips away from the food as it cooks, it renders fat, resulting in a healthier dish overall. Grilling cooks food evenly and prevents it from drying out, as long as you turn it in every few minutes. It does not overheat the fats or oils, which can cause carcinogens to form. Frying, on the other hand, can result in dangerously high temperatures, resulting in unwanted and potentially dangerous by-products. When you grill food, you add flavor by caramelizing the natural sugars in the meat (a process known as the Maillard reaction), which gives it that delicious "barbecue" flavor. Furthermore, grilling produces a less greasy product by rendering excess fat while keeping the juice. Grilling will change the way you think about food if you have the time and resources. The flavor is out of this world, and with the right meat marinades or cuts, as well as a squeeze of the citrus afterward, both vegetables and meats can be transformed under the grill. Grilling is also less messy. When preparing a delicious meal for the family, we all have to know how many dishes we actually use. Let's face it; no one enjoys doing dishes. When you're grilling your favorite dish, you don't have to be concerned about getting all pans dirty. But The grill is simple to clean. With a wood scraper, you may get it absolutely hot so that the unwanted leftovers burn off.

Made in the USA
Middletown, DE
16 December 2021

56253293R00044